Fingernail Moon:
A Coalcracker looks for Glassboro

by Ben Jezierski

Fingernail Moon: A Coalcracker Looks for Glassboro

Published by Putting It on the Wind Press

ISBN: 979-8-9947202-0-2

Cover design by Ben Jezierski

Interior design by Ben Jezierski

Printed in the United States of America

For the One who sends the words -
and the one who provides the space
in which to write them...

This is how
we come to know
one another:

statue by statue;
leaf by leaf;
fragments of ourselves,
gathered and assembled
into quiet initiations
of discovery.

Introduction:

Imagine that you live in a small but productive coal mining town in what today is commonly known as the Mid Valley region of Northeastern Pennsylvania. Like most of the men and capable boys in your neighborhood, you earn your living in the Anthracite mine that undergirds the length and breadth of the ground beneath your feet. The work is dangerous and difficult, but as long as there are sons or brothers to lower into it, that hole in the ground will continue to provide the roof over your head and the food on your table.

You return home one evening, tired, sore, swaddled in soot, pretty much the same way you and your next-door neighbor have done countless times before. Brothers almost since childhood, you've wept shoulder to shoulder at family funerals in the pews at Saint Mary's Church, and celebrated the births of each other's children. You've eaten together, and staggered home together from the Company-owned bar down the street. You've fed each other's families with vegetables from the gardens you've planted in the common yard behind your houses. And you've labored together in the dark and the damp for more years than either of you would even care to remember.

Every morning, side by side, you've made your way to the mine. Every evening, side by side, you've made your way back home. On this particular evening, however, you stand in front of your neighbor's house alone. Earlier today, he was working the cramped and narrow confines of a monkey vein. The ceiling shifted, and now this man, whose dusty laughter rattled the windows of Breaker Street, lies crushed and buried beneath the tons of earth and rock that killed him. There's nothing left for the Black Mariah to carry, and so it falls to you to deliver the news to his newly-widowed wife and his children.

The life depicted here was never mine. But its cultural legacy and mythic inheritance are with me to this day. By the time I was born, little remained of the coal mining industry but skeletal breakers, ubiquitous culm banks, and the occasional rotten-egg smell of a still-active mine fire on the wind.

To some, this might sound ominous, or maybe even depressing, but for one particularly inquisitive child, who spent his days picking fossils and roaming the sparse Gray Birch copses dotting those same culm banks, it fostered a deep and personal connection with the Spirit of the place. From the minute my bare feet left the linoleum and found themselves on grass and shale, I ran with it. I breathed it in, and felt its hand against my cheek in the mystery of every breeze. It offered something that the chaos of a household riven by alcohol, poverty, and emotional instability could not - it offered a deep and unshakable sense of home.

As I write these words, I am sixty-two years old. Many years ago, I traded the culm banks and Company houses of a small Northeastern Pennsylvania borough for the stockade fences and manicured lawns of a suburban vinyl village in Southern New Jersey, only to discover within myself a kind of spiritual homelessness.

The following work chronicles an attempt, if not to cure this condition, then at least, perhaps, to alleviate it. These poems are the result of a year-long endeavor to establish contact with the Spirit of another place, to make myself available to its idiosyncrasies and its graces, and if it so desired, to share with it a few of my own. I'll let these words stand as proof of the degree to which we were both forthcoming in our efforts...

January 2026
Ben Jezierski, Author
Glassboro, New Jersey
bjezierski1@yahoo.com

2/26

The Cherry trees
in the Rite Aid parking lot
are dark and stunted;
resulting,
no doubt,
from a steady diet
of exhaust fumes;
and yet,
they somehow manage
to find the necessary gumption
to survive.

Not much of an observation
to be sure,
but it's one that comes to mind
on this first,
warm,
evening walk
of the year.

In the empty field across the street,
the echoes
of last year's grass
brush against the soles
of my walking shoes,
mingle with the crunch of leaves,
and whither once again
into silence.

Despite the warmer
than average temperature,
there's an obvious chill in the air,
but it's slight enough
to find itself
easily kept at bay
by a brisk pace
and a light woolen shirt,
buttoned at the waist.

As I get out
towards the more expensive homes,
I catch the faintest whiff
of chimney smoke;
little more than a nuance really,
but reminder enough
that we're not yet done
with winter...

2/29

I pull on my gloves
and round the corner
past the lighted garages
on Sienna.

It's cold tonight;
bitter, actually,
so, it feels more like winter
than almost spring.

There's still a trace
of blue in the sky,
and a handful of stars
sneaking their way
past the orange glow
of the streetlights.

It's a perfect night for a walk;
and despite the occasional passing car
and the random music in my earbuds,
a palpable silence rises up
and drapes itself
over everything.

Soon there'll be lawn mowers,
tightly clustered groups of dog walkers,
and young kids
playing basketball
in the streets.

But for now, it's gloves
and traces of blue,
and a solitary combing
through the last
few
resistant knots
of winter...

03/03

Tonight, my shoes
are calling the shots,
and I am simply tagging along
for the ride.

The neighborhood is safe
and well-lit,
so, they're pretty much free
to wander wherever they choose.

Walking the Earth,
listening to the music of the sole;
it's been like this
ever since I was old enough
to understand
just how necessary that could be.

I love this space,
the internal one
that opens up
and gives me room to breathe;
allows in the occasional detail,
just to keep me grounded:
the twisting of a root,
the metallic whine
of a power tool in the distance,
the rush and hum of the traffic
out on Delsea.

But sometimes
it's something a bit more tangible:
a feather perhaps,
or a pine cone,
or a few stray words,
echoing
long after my shoes and I
have settled down
for the evening...

03/11

The lawns are littered
with broken twigs
and the occasional plastic water bottle.

All last night
and most of today
the wind prowled the streets,
shaking trees
and kicking over garbage cans.

It follows me now,
cold and almost constant,
beneath a fingernail moon
and a cloudless sky
of iron-blue
and green…

03/13

"Don't push the river,"
he thinks to himself,
and soon the words
come rushing in on their own.

Seconds before
he'd wrestled with pastel clouds
and last year's leaves
strewn about the lawns
like discarded candy wrappers.

Yesterday's winds
were far from kind
with some of the older trees,
and their limbs and branches
lay bundled and stacked,
ready for tomorrow's pickup.

He rests within these images for a while,
allowing the words
to present themselves
only when they're ready;
when not three paces in front of him,
the first gray squirrel of the season
jumps the curb
and lopes its way
across the concrete sidewalk...

03/18

On Charles III
I adjust my scarf,
zip my jacket,
and lean into the wind.

Every step is blossoms
and the dry-bone rattle
of dead leaves
along the asphalt.

The setting sun
brushes the clouds
with orange,
pink,
and gold;

and the daffodils stagger,
mouths agape,
awestruck
at the mystery of it all...

03/29

Hastas and tulips,
daffodils and dandelions,
fresh-cut lawns,
and the smell
of drying laundry.

The birdsongs
are more prevalent these days.

And now and then
the chattering of neighbors
mingles
with the plaintive peal of wind chimes,
suspended among
the newly budding branches.

The ghosts of winter have all but gone,
and yet,
there's a certain stubbornness
to the chill
that hones the ever-shifting breeze.

The orchard doesn't seem to notice,
and neither do the Dogwoods;
only the contemplative poet,
marking his time
in footsteps and phrases,
dares to pay it any heed at all...

04/12

Backyard Buddhas,
dandelions,
tulips,
and an endless parade
of middle-aged men
behind lawnmowers.

I love these evening walks
around the neighborhood;
especially now
that everything
is finally waking up.

The clover on the corner
is ankle-deep,
and the patches of brown
in the front yard
are beginning to disappear.

Even though
we're a few days out
from frigid mornings
and layers of frost
on the windshields of our cars,
it's starting to feel
as if there's no going back.

I sense a little something of that
inside myself these days;
fingers of green,
brushing aside the remnants
of last year's leaves...

04/24

Greens and yellows,
purples
and flashes of white;

even in the fading light,
the plants
continue to remind me
that we've made it past
the mottled grays
of winter.

Edges softened
by new growth,
the sidewalk
feels a little friendlier;

and Cherries and Dogwoods
drift like painted smoke
amidst the incessant whispering
of the leaves...

04/26

The dandelions
have gone to seed
in the uncut grass along Sienna.

Over on Forest,
Clematis storms the mailboxes.

I walk the loop,
beckoned by the baby-pinks
and harlot-reds of Azaleas,
shamelessly plying their trade
between the Boxwoods.

There's a subtle awareness
in these evening walks
that's deepened
as I've gotten older:

awareness
of a palpable familiarity:

familiarity
of a young and solitary child
reading in the crook of a Dogwood tree:

reading out loud to the tree itself;

recognizing,
down in his bones,
the watchful attention
of a necessary presence...

05/06

Most of the lawns
are manicured,
and a green
that only comes
with modern chemistry.

Here,
they strive
for monoculture.

It's quite a contrast
with my own yard,
and its healthy crop
of plantain and crabgrass.
The clover's rampant,
so, it's usually thick
with honeybees.

There's also a garden,
and while it might not
resemble Innisfree,
there's still a sense
of peace that comes
from being there.

The Cardinals make their rain songs
as I duck beneath
the laden branches
of an Oak tree.

It's humid now,
and the storm
will likely be here
sooner than later...

05/13

At the corner of Vermillion,
a line of trees
blocks the sun
and creates
the false appearances
of twilight.

We're deep into spring,
and these evening walks
carry me from places
where patches of clover
erupt like stars
against a sky of green.

The sounds of yardwork,
Oak Leaf Hydrangea,
the chattering of birds,
and the flick
of a gray squirrel's tail;
the swish of grass
beneath my feet
where Arbor Vitae
claim their half
of the sidewalk.

I'm an old man,
talking to himself
in the midst of it;
painting it all
with words
and the spaces between...

05/22

Sprinklers
and manicured lawns,
razor-edged
along the walkways,
pallets of mulch,
and variegated Hastas.

Down by the creek
the wild Primrose
flashes white
through knots
of leafy green.

I share my walk
with Robins and Grackles,
the occasional Mockingbird,
and Cardinals singing rain
from the tops of the trees.

The breeze is cool
and nearly constant,
and a bank of clouds
obscures the Western sky.

It's good
to be surrounded
by these things,
to breathe them in,
and feel them mingle
with the ever-present sweetness
of their passing...

06/03

These
are the kind
of streets you can cross
without looking.

There's not a lot of traffic,
and what there is
usually gives itself away
a couple of blocks
before it closes in.

It's quiet here;
and if you really stop to listen,
you can hear the Hastas
whispering in their beds.

Oak Leaf Hydrangeas,
Marigolds, and Petunias
shamelessly devour
the last few scraps of sunlight;
but the Peonies
are getting drowsy,
so, they linger,
bellies full
and on the verge of sleep...

06/24

Tonight
it's broken branches
and cooler weather.

My neighbor and I
chat for a bit,
and he calls me over
to talk about
the Maple tree he's planted.

We've both been busy lately,
and it feels good
to stop
and take some time.

Shortly afterwards,
I find a Crow feather
in the grass beneath an Oak.
I pick it up
and make an offering.
It's been a while
since someone left me a feather.

As I finish my walk,
my next-door neighbor
greets me again,
and we exchange
a couple of laughs.
Back inside,
I smudge the feather
and place it on my altar.

There's a feeling of acceptance
in all of this...

07/02

I get pulled onto Forest
by unseen hands,
cross the street,
and continue around the bend.

These evenings
come equipped with revelation;
and the walking
is essentially
at the heart of it.

A stray leaf,
pasted against a mailbox;

a familiar statue
in someone's yard,
chipped
and disregarded
long ago;

and tonight,
a Mullein plant
steps around,
and beckons me
from its hiding place
behind a Scarlet Oak.

This is how
we come to know
one another:

statue by statue;
leaf by leaf;
fragments of ourselves,
gathered and assembled
into quiet initiations
of discovery...

07/19

The Crepe Myrtle looms
against the vinyl siding,
spilling shadow
over crab grass
and plantain.

My thoughts and I
are out here again,
dodging squirrels
amidst
the sunburned Hastas.

Occasionally
we stop and chat
with the neighbors;
but the rabbits
will tolerate
just so much of it,
so, our words are brief,
and fade
like ragged church bells
in the distance...

08/12

It's all
beginning to feel
a little bit older.

The grass that struggled
through the lingering heat
of summer
now stands half a foot;
and dying flowers,
petals rumpled and brown,
hang in the air
like passing fireworks.

This is green time:
not the brightly innocent
green of spring,
but a deeper green,
that whispers softly
of rust.

It carries Elder wisdom
in its heart,
and speaks of gold
and auburn yet to come...

09/03

The sunset
brings a coolness
to the evening.

The Mugwort
is everywhere these days,
and doesn't seem to notice
the change in temperature.

Song-birds gossip
about their summers,
and huddle together in the twilight,
dreaming of longer days
and warmer nights.

There's still a little purple
near the mailboxes,
and flashes of yellow,
giving way to gold.

The crackle of acorns
beneath my feet
is nearly constant now.

And soon the Oaks
will fold away
the greens
of spring and summer,
and wrap themselves
in oranges,
reds,
and umbers...

09/26

Even the chemically-treated lawns
have given up the ghost.

The grass is tired now,
and draws up
threadbare sheets of green
across its aching feet.

Among the pine needles
the fallen leaves
offer little
in the way of comfort;
brittle and dry
as the nearly silent wind
that whispers,

"Rain..."

And yet
Impatiens gird the mailboxes,
blissfully unaware
of what surrounds them;
or perhaps,
they understand it all too well,
so, they tear themselves completely apart,
and offer up
one final
splash
of pink...

10/10

The air
is dipped
in Autumn tonight.

The Maple tree
in the front yard
is aflame
with reds and oranges;
and half-a-moon
hangs
silver and white
in an otherwise
unbroken evening sky.

Each step carries me
further away
from the greens
and pinks of summer;
while the dry leaves
beneath my feet
speak gently
the eulogies of their lives...

10/25

Out here
fishing for words again
amidst the fallen leaves,
the bone-dry grass,
and the threadbare
inflatable pumpkins.

The ghosts of summer
cling to the trees,
trading used-to-be greens
for the all-to-relevant immediacy
of reds and browns.

There's beauty here,
in this world of dying leaves.
It rises up
and spills out
in the shape of letters
from the cold
and stoney ground...

10/28

A rabbit breaks the shadows,
slicing through the grass
in front of the house.

The wind and the drought
have taken most of the leaves;
scattered them
across the brittle lawns,
or left them gathered
in mass graves
along the curb.

Too warm,
too cold,
and the distance in between
are written
in the pages
of these days.

Everything seems to move
a little bit slower.

It sits back,
stretches
and yawns;
presses on
to finish
these last few lines...

11/02

The air is crisp
and begs a heavier shirt.

The evening opens graciously,
draws me deep inside itself,
and wraps me
in a tangible familiarity.

Not the familiarity
of recent times,
but that of my younger days,
and the soulful magic
of those long
and lonely midnight walks
back home.

I welcome these things;
feel them swell
within some part of me
that reaches out
and brushes against
the Spirit of this place...

11/11

A half-mast moon
throws shadows
at 11 o'clock.

The sound of a train
off in the distance,
and the crush of leaves
beneath my feet,
speak of something stirring
in the midst of it.

A broken stick,
an uneven sidewalk,
the smoker's cough
of an engine
out on Delsea:
unwanted clutter
at times, perhaps;
but in this moment,
more the thing itself
than distraction from it...

11/25

Everything's a little bit softer
now that the drought is broken.

Phantom greens
wrestle with browns and yellows
in the all-but-dormant grass.

Mounds of dampened Oak leaves
clog the sides of the street,
nipping the edges of the breeze
with tea and sugar.

I meet the chill
wearing a couple of Tee-shirts
and a light jacket.
It walks along beside me;
reaches for my hand,
and we pause for a moment
beneath the boughs of a Maple,
warmed by the glow
of Autumn's dying embers...

12/08

Fast food onions
and Christmas lights;
the crackle of leaves,
and a breeze
that tells me
I probably should've worn
a heavier coat.

We're sweeping up
the remnants of Autumn;
getting ready
for a winter
of greens and grays.

Amidst the twinkling hedges,
an anachronistic lawn sprinkler
stands its ground;

the last of summer's pickets,
refusing to surrender its post...

12/18

The air is thick
with the promise of rain,
but the blacktop shimmers
as if it's already fallen.

They're burning steak
in the strip mall
out on Delsea.

The constant brush of traffic
and the whisper of wind
through dry leaves
is the soundtrack
for the evening.

The parking lot
is nearly vacant,
and the storefronts
smile gap-toothed
as I make my way back home
from the bank.

The rain fulfills its promise
with a block-and-a-half to go,
but my shoes don't seem to notice;
or if they do,
perhaps they just don't care.

And so, we take our time,
my shoes and I,
drawing out
these last few minutes
of our journey...

12/23

Flickering lights
splash the ragged canvas
of the snow
like watercolors,
spilt carelessly
and left to run.

The shadows of branches
crack the sidewalks,
and my own
steps lightly among them
for fear of falling...

12/30

My feet turn left
at the end
of the driveway.

As the road bends,
Orion
leaps across my path,
and comes to rest
in a patch of sky
as fraught with stars
as the rooftops
and the bushes
along Persimmon.

Winter indulges itself
in the denial
of lighter clothing;
though the trees see fit
to stand naked
in the truth of it...

1/9

Patches of blue-gray snow
fleck the grass
beneath a moon
so bright
it summons shadow.

The air is clear,
and cuts through skin
like broken window glass.

The ghosts of Autumn
dog my footsteps,
and curl about the gutters;
their brittle voices,
intermingling
with the rumble of a jet,
and the constant hum of traffic
in the distance...

1/12

The fractal branches
of naked trees
snapshot
last year's growth;
simultaneously capturing
stillness and motion.

They occupy,
and yet suggest,
their space.

Arthritic limbs
and the implications
of leaves;
cold fingers,
clutching at clouds
and scattering stars...

1/29

The well-honed chill
of a January breeze
tatters gloves
and freezes words
as soon as they appear.

Stars and streetlights
punctuate the sky,
shattering
the cobalt blue
of the coming night.

The ghosts of windchimes
rattle the porches,
and dogs cry out
for attention;
and somewhere on Delsea
the pulse of a siren
and the plaintive rasp
of an engine
calling me home...

2/3

An unexpected
right-hand turn
puts me out
on Vermillion;
on nights like this,
my feet
have a mind
of their own.

They carry me
past the tidy mailboxes
and well-lit homes
with front lawns
patched and thread-bare;
last year's blankets,
fraying at the edge.

There's traffic,
and the hiss of leaves,
and the scuff of shoes
against a concrete sidewalk.

It settles in
and speaks its piece
through cul-de-sacs
and car horns:
the domesticated whisperings
of its song...

2/11

Tonight, the crunch
of falling snow
blurs the edges,
and insulates my thoughts.

It gathers on my jacket
and in my hood,
unbreaks the sidewalks,
and wraps the usual
neighborhood sounds
in silence.

It brushes dreamlike
across the landscape,
and a thought arises
or perhaps,
more accurately,
a feeling
that I am simply wandering
through the dreams
of something
other than myself;

something that sleeps
in the vestibules
of mailboxes,
and whispers its name
amidst the soft,
dark,
murmuring
of storm drains...

Author's note

Walk through our back yard on any given day - when the crazy-quilt assortment of crabgrass, sorrel, plantain, clover, and dandelions that passes for a lawn is healthy and at its peak, and you are likely to notice small clusters of faint, yet clearly defined circular patches. There were orchards on these lands before the builders cut them down, and although the physical remains of those trees lay buried beneath an almost-ceramic layer of development soil, their presence continues to bleed through.

Over the last few years, I'd begun to view the entire neighborhood through the lens of this idea: that somewhere, beneath the facade of vinyl-sided uniformity and ubiquitous Hastas, lay something that refused to disappear; something wild and untamable...bleeding through.

This work, born from a deep sense of spiritual homelessness, has been my humble attempt to venture out and, if permitted, to encounter that something on whatever terms it offered. I've returned from this journey with a feeling of acknowledgement, and an awareness that I have finally come home...

www.ingramcontent.com/pod-product-compliance
Lightning Source LLC
LaVergne TN
LVHW090537110826
845146LV00003B/1152

* 9 7 9 8 9 9 4 7 2 0 2 0 2 *